AMERICA'S STRUGGLE with TERRORISM

BY MARK FRIEDMAN

CHILDREN'S PRESS®

An Imprint of Scholastic Inc.

New York   Toronto   London   Auckland   Sydney
Mexico City   New Delhi   Hong Kong
Danbury, Connecticut

BRINGING HISTORY to LIFE

Content Consultant
Christopher Gelpi, PhD
Professor of Political Science
Duke University
Charlotte, North Carolina

Library of Congress Cataloging-in-Publication Data

Friedman, Mark, 1963–
   America's struggle with terrorism/by Mark Friedman.
      p. cm.—(Cornerstones of freedom)
   Includes bibliographical references and index.
   ISBN-13: 978-0-531-25026-6 (lib. bdg.)   ISBN-10: 0-531-25026-1 (lib. bdg.)
   ISBN-13: 978-0-531-26551-2 (pbk.)   ISBN-10: 0-531-26551-X (pbk.)
   1. Terrorism—United States—Juvenile literature. 2. Terrorism—United
States—History—Juvenile literature. I. Title.
   HV6432.F743 2011
   363.3250973—dc22   2011015939

Printed in the United States of America 113
SCHOLASTIC, CHILDREN'S PRESS, CORNERSTONES OF FREEDOM™,
and associated logos are trademarks and/or registered trademarks of
Scholastic Inc.

1 2 3 4 5 6 7 8 9 10 R 21 20 19 18 17 16 15 14 13 12

Photographs © 2012: AP Images: 28 (David Caulkin), 24 (Bob Dear),
30 (Eric Draper, The White House), 44 (Richard Drew), 7 (Hillery Smith
Garrison), 47 (Joshua Gunter/The Plain Dealer), 35 (Ron Heflin), 37 (Justice
Department), 38 (KFOR-TV/Cable News Network), 32, 39, 52 (David
Longstreath), 5 bottom, 12, 15 bottom (North Wind Picture Archives),
48, 53 top (Carmen Taylor), back cover, 4 bottom, 34, 36, 45, 46, 57 top,
57 bottom; Corbis Images: 26 (Bettmann), 31 (Bryn Colton/Assignments
Photographers), 29 (Wally McNamee), 42 (Michel Setboun); Getty Images:
20 (Tim Boyle), 49 (Doug Kanter/AFP), 41 (Arthur Lien/AFP), 50 (Rich Lipski/
Washington Post), 23 (NY Daily News Archive), cover (Lyle Owerko), 2, 3,
54 (Jonathan Saruk); International Institute of Social History, Amsterdam:
22; Landov, LLC: 6, 59 (Geoff Green), 40 (Ronald Martinez/Reuters); Library
of Congress: 5 top, 21 (Harris & Ewing), 14, 58 (H.H. Lloyd & Co.), 13, 56
(Small, Maynard, & Company), 8, 10, 15 top, 53 bottom; Mark Friedman: 64;
Superstock, Inc.: 4 top, 16 (Everett Collection), 18 (Pantheon).

Did you know that studying history can be fun?

BRING HISTORY TO LIFE by becoming a history investigator. Examine the evidence (primary and secondary source materials); cross-examine the people and witnesses. Take a look at what was happening at the time—but be careful! What happened years ago might suddenly become incredibly interesting and change the way you think!

Contents

Terror Comes to America

The deadliest terrorist attack in U.S. history took place on September 11, 2001.

Terrorists unleashed a violent attack on the United States on the morning of September 11, 2001. Coordinated groups of terrorists boarded four ordinary airplanes. Two were in Boston, Massachusetts. One was in Washington, D.C. The last was in Newark, New Jersey. The terrorists took control of the airplanes soon after they took off and deliberately crashed them. Two planes crashed into the World Trade Center towers in New York City. One crashed into the Pentagon near Washington, D.C. The fourth crashed in a field in rural Pennsylvania after passengers fought to overpower the terrorists and divert the plane from its target. More than 3,000 people were dead by the time the smoke cleared. More than 6,000 others were injured.

Why would terrorists attack a nation in this way? The definition of *terrorism* varies wildly depending on the source. But all terrorists share some traits. Terrorists' goals are usually political or religious. They work to achieve these goals by using violence, fear, and threats. Their attacks are intended to force change by scaring the targets into giving in. These attacks generally harm civilians. But government or military targets can also be victims of terrorism.

The attacks on 9/11 caused major damage to the Pentagon.

ATTACK IN THE UNITED STATES.

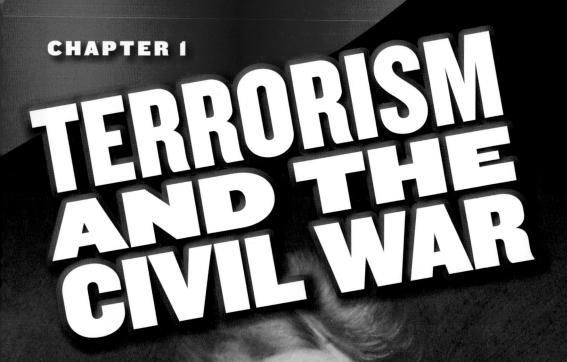

CHAPTER 1

TERRORISM AND THE CIVIL WAR

John Brown became known as the Father of American Terrorism.

AMERICANS STILL FEAR POTENTIAL terrorist attacks by people from other nations more than a decade after 9/11. But terrorists born in the United States are also a threat. U.S. history has been marked by many examples of American citizens carrying out terrorist attacks against other Americans.

John Brown and his men used violence in an attempt to end slavery.

John Brown's Anger

The United States was divided on the issue of slavery in the mid-1800s. Most people in Southern states believed that white people had the right to own slaves. But a growing number of people in the North objected to the idea of slavery. These **abolitionists** believed that slavery should be illegal.

John Brown was a white abolitionist. He committed several acts of violence against supporters of slavery. Brown wanted to start a war to free the slaves. He led a gang in an attack on a pro-slavery group in Kansas in 1856. Brown's gang killed five men in the attack.

Raid on Harpers Ferry

John Brown escaped punishment for the Kansas attack and continued to recruit abolitionists for his fight to end slavery. In 1859, he decided to attack the U.S. government in order to inspire a slave revolt and start a war.

On the night of October 16, 1859, Brown led a band of 21 men in a raid on the U.S. military armory at Harpers Ferry, Virginia. The gang stole weapons, took **hostages**, and gained control of the armory. The raid was shocking. But Brown failed to inspire a slave revolt. U.S. Marines attacked Harpers Ferry the next day. They wounded Brown, killed 10 of his gang, and retook the armory.

A Terrorist's Impact

John Brown has been called the Father of American Terrorism. His raid did not immediately spark the war he desired. But his violent actions did inspire others to take

President Lincoln's leadership helped the Union achieve victory in the Civil War.

up the antislavery cause. Many historians agree that his raid on Harpers Ferry was one of the key events leading to the American Civil War (1861–1865).

President Abraham Lincoln guided the United States through the war, which threatened to split the nation apart. Lincoln's intense commitment to reuniting the two halves of the country kept the Union focused when the Southern Confederacy appeared to be gaining an upper hand. Lincoln issued the Emancipation Proclamation in 1863. It freed all slaves in Confederate states.

Confederate Assassins

The Civil War ended with the Confederacy's surrender in 1865. With this defeat came an end to slavery. This result greatly angered many Southerners.

One man who could not accept the defeat was John Wilkes Booth. Booth was an actor from the slave state of Maryland. His hatred of Abraham Lincoln grew as he watched the Confederacy fall apart. He began scheming to kidnap the president. But he changed his plan to murder after the war ended. Booth plotted with three other men to **assassinate** not only President Lincoln, but also Vice President Andrew Johnson and Secretary of State William Seward. This plan would eliminate the three most powerful leaders of the U.S. government all at one time.

TODAY'S PERSPECTIVE

Today, Americans agree that slavery was a horrible practice. It is easy for modern people to admire John Brown's courage and determination to end slavery, but it is also important to remember that he acted as a terrorist. He worked with a band of other people, planned a coordinated attack, and attempted to use violence to disrupt society. Terrorists use violence to protest the wrongs they see in society. But there are nonviolent ways for them to communicate their ideas as well.

Booth was able to get close to Lincoln because Lincoln's bodyguard had left his post outside the presidential box.

On the night of April 14, 1865, President Lincoln and his wife, Mary, attended a play at Ford's Theatre in Washington, D.C. Booth worked at the theater as an actor. He was able to move throughout the building freely. He sneaked into Lincoln's private box during the play and shot him in the head. He then leaped down to the stage and shouted to all in attendance, "I have done it, the South is avenged!"

Booth's partners were not as successful in completing their parts of the plan. Lewis Powell managed to enter Seward's home and stab him several times. But he was quickly tackled to the ground. Seward was able to survive the attack. Another partner in the plot grew too frightened to take part. He went to the hotel where Johnson was staying. But he got drunk at the hotel bar instead of killing the vice president.

Abraham Lincoln died from the gunshot wound the next morning as John Wilkes Booth fled from Washington, D.C. Booth was tracked down and shot by U.S. soldiers. Booth had succeeded in killing the president. But he had failed to create terror in the United States. The nation became more unified in its sorrow over its fallen leader.

Most Americans saw Lincoln's death as a tragedy.

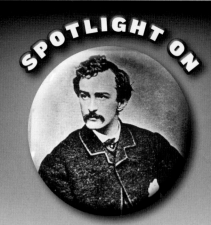

SPOTLIGHT ON

John Wilkes Booth

John Wilkes Booth was born on May 10, 1838, to a family of well-known actors. He began his own acting career in 1858 and soon found success performing in Shakespeare's plays in Southern states during the Civil War. Booth was a strong believer in slavery. He was part of the militia group that captured and killed John Brown in 1859.

After shooting Lincoln, Booth fled to Virginia. On April 26, 1865, U.S. troops found him hiding in a barn, which they set on fire. Booth refused to surrender. He was shot and killed.

CHAPTER 2

ANARCHISTS IN THE USA

...en!

MASS-MEETING

TO-NIGHT, at 7.30 o'clock,

===== AT THE =====

HAYMARKET, Randolph St., Bet. Desplaines and Halste

Good Speakers will be present to denounce the late atrocious act of the police, the shooting of our fellow-workmen yesterday afternoon.

Workingmen Arm Yourselves and Appear in Full Force!

THE EXECUTIVE COMMITTE

Achtung, Arbeiter!

Große

In the 19th century, many workers fought for better treatment.

Massen-Versammlun

Heute Abend '8 Uhr auf

SLAVERY WAS NOT THE ONLY source of tension in 19th-century America. Another conflict emerged in the late 1800s as workers demanded greater rights from employers. More and more people were working in factories run by large companies. These workers struggled with dangerous working conditions, low pay, and long hours. Protests for workers' rights eventually led to violent terrorist acts.

The Haymarket Riot

Leaders of the **labor movement** fought against a system in which millions of workers suffered while a small number of business owners got rich. Some members of the movement wanted to kick out the managers who controlled factories and allow workers to set their own rules.

Loud protests for workers' rights began occurring across the country. Thousands of Chicago workers went on strike in April and early May 1886 to demand an 8-hour workday rather than the 12- or 14-hour days that many jobs required. The protests grew violent as the crowds swelled. Police struck back. They shot and

The Haymarket meeting led to an outbreak of violence.

A FIRSTHAND LOOK AT
HAYMARKET FLYERS

Early flyers advertising the Haymarket protest encouraged workingmen to bring weapons and "appear in full force." A second batch of flyers removed these words because one of the speakers refused to talk if violence was encouraged. See page 60 for links to view the flyers online.

killed several protesters. At a May 4 protest in the city's Haymarket district, 176 police officers moved in to break up the gathering.

Somebody threw a bomb at the police. Chaos ensued. The police opened fire on the protesters. Many people were killed in the battle that followed. Seven police officers also died. Hundreds of protesters were injured.

Anarchists on Trial

Nobody ever discovered who threw the bomb that ignited the Haymarket Riot. But police did learn that **anarchists** were involved in organizing the workers' protests. Some anarchists seek to change society by disrupting the ways in which business, government, and ordinary life usually run. Eight anarchists were put on trial for the Haymarket Riot and convicted of murder. Four of them were put to death by hanging on November 11, 1887. Years later, government officials recognized that the trial was unfair. The men who had been hanged were probably punished for crimes they did not commit.

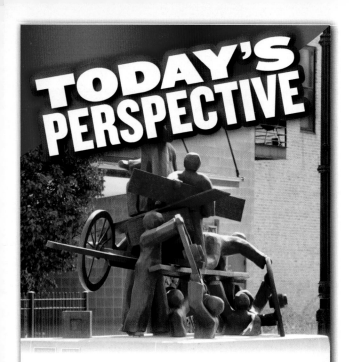

TODAY'S PERSPECTIVE

Today, a memorial sculpture stands at the intersection of Desplaines and Lake Streets in Chicago, where the Haymarket Riot took place. Sculptor Mary Brogger created the memorial in 2004. It depicts protesters standing on a wooden wagon, just as they were at the moment when the bomb exploded. The sculpture commemorates the protesters and the important cause they were supporting. Today, workers' rights are protected under laws that came about partly because of violent protests such as the Haymarket Riot.

Targeting Leaders

American anarchists launched a bombing campaign against well-known politicians and business leaders in April 1919. Thirty plainly wrapped packages were sent to prominent Americans such as Supreme Court justice Oliver Wendell Holmes and businessman John D. Rockefeller. Only a couple of these bombs reached their destinations. Nobody was killed.

Italian anarchist Luigi Galleani staged a bombing attack on eight U.S. cities in June. His organization exploded powerful bombs directly in front of eight homes. One target was the attorney general of the United States, A. Mitchell Palmer. Palmer and his family were not injured. But the bomber blew himself up,

A. Mitchell Palmer's home was damaged in a terrorist attack.

possibly by tripping over the bomb. Each of the eight bombs was sent with a note that read, "There will have to be bloodshed; we will not dodge; there will have to be murder: we will kill, because it is necessary; we will . . . rid the world of your tyrannical institutions."

Palmer launched an effort to find and get rid of anarchists and **communists** in the United States. The Palmer Raids resulted in more than 500 foreign citizens being arrested and **deported**.

Luigi Galleani

Luigi Galleani was born in Italy. He first took an interest in anarchy while attending college. He was forced to leave Italy in 1880 to avoid arrest. He spent time in France and Switzerland, where he met with other anarchists and organized protests.

Galleani moved to the United States in 1901 and began working at an anarchist newspaper. His writing and public speaking skills soon gained him a group of followers known as Galleanists. After being deported in June 1919, Galleani returned to Italy, where police kept a close eye on him for the rest of his life.

Terror Strikes Wall Street

Luigi Galleani was deported. But the anarchist bombings in the United States did not cease. On September 16, 1920, a tremendous explosion rocked the streets of New York's financial district. Someone had driven a horse-drawn wagon into the center of the district and set off 100 pounds (45 kilograms) of dynamite and 500 pounds (225 kg) of iron slugs. The slugs became tiny missiles. They cut through walls and injured hundreds of people. One witness said that a wall of fire rose 10 stories above the street. Thirty people died in the attack. Nine more died later from their injuries.

The direct target of the attack appeared to be the headquarters of J. P. Morgan. J. P. Morgan was one of the most powerful banking companies in the world. Morgan himself was not in the office that day. But flying glass injured several bank officers. The offices were severely damaged. Most of the deaths and injuries were suffered by innocent bystanders on the street.

A note found the next day claimed that "American Anarchist Fighters" were responsible. The anarchists' identities remained a mystery. But their actions succeeded in creating panic. No one was ever arrested for the attack.

The Wall Street bombing in 1920 killed 30 people.

CHAPTER 3

FOREIGN TERRORISTS AND AMERICA

In the 1970s, the foreign policy of the United States made it an enemy of Iran.

THE POWER AND INFLUENCE

of the United States grew throughout the world during the 20th century. U.S. military and business dealings in foreign countries created new allies and new enemies. Few enemies had the military strength to wage war against the United States. Instead, some used terrorism to strike at American citizens living and working in foreign lands.

The rocky relationship between the United States and Iran led to many Americans being taken hostage.

The Iran Hostage Crisis

The United States had a close and friendly relationship with the shah of Iran, Mohammad Reza Pahlavi, in the 1970s. He was the country's longtime ruler. Then, in January 1979, the shah's opponents in Iran overthrew him in a revolt. The shah left Iran. Ayatollah Khomeini took control of the nation. The ayatollah was a religious leader who installed a government of strict Islamic rule.

The shah was allowed to enter the United States in October 1979 for cancer treatment at the Mayo Clinic in Minnesota. The people of Iran were outraged. They wanted the shah to be put on trial in Iran for various crimes. In response, some Iranians targeted Americans working at the embassy in Iran's capital city, Tehran.

On November 4, 1979, a group of armed Iranian students stormed the embassy and took the 66 Americans there as hostages. The ayatollah supported the students. They demanded that the United States return the shah to Iran and hand over billions of dollars as well.

The American Response

U.S. president Jimmy Carter responded to the crisis by imposing an oil **embargo**. The United States would no longer buy oil from Iran. Iran would not receive American payments. This was meant to cripple the Iranian economy. But the embargo produced few results. The ayatollah released a small number of hostages but kept 52 in captivity.

The hostage crisis dragged on for months. Americans

A FIRSTHAND LOOK AT
AN INTERVIEW WITH BARRY ROSEN

One of the hostages spoke to a CNN reporter about what it was like to spend 444 days in captivity. "The 444 days were unendurable. . . . Iranians treated us in the most horrendous way possible. . . . They certainly did put fear into my heart." See page 60 for a link to read the entire interview online.

The hostages celebrated as they were released from captivity.

demanded strong action to bring the captives home. Six months into the crisis, President Carter authorized a U.S. military rescue mission that resulted in disaster. Several helicopters malfunctioned. One crashed, resulting in the deaths of eight Americans. Iran rejoiced, and Americans were distraught.

After 444 days, the hostage crisis ended at the very moment Carter's presidency ended. He lost the presidential election to Ronald Reagan in November 1980. Just as Reagan took office on January 20, 1981, Iran released the hostages. They returned to a hero's welcome in the United States.

Beirut Embassy Bombings

The Iran hostage crisis showed governments and other groups around the world that they could wound the United States with terror. The crisis was followed by a decade of violence against Americans around the world. Another U.S. embassy was targeted by a **suicide bomber** in 1983.

In the Middle East, a military conflict between U.S. ally Israel and several Arab nations had been raging for decades. Lebanon was

YESTERDAY'S HEADLINES

The Iran hostage crisis inspired a new form of news coverage on American television. ABC News began airing a late-night news program called *Nightline* early in the hostage crisis. Each episode opened with the title "America Held Hostage: Day 10" (the number would change each day). The program allowed a single, important news topic to be covered in-depth for 30 minutes. It was a new concept at the time. *Nightline* is still running more than 30 years later.

a hotbed for anti-Israeli groups such as Hezbollah, which used terrorist tactics to fight Israel. On April 18, 1983, a van loaded with 2,000 pounds (900 kg) of explosives barreled through the security barriers at the U.S. Embassy in Beirut, Lebanon. The van crashed into the front lobby of the building. The driver then set off the explosives, killing himself

TODAY'S PERSPECTIVE

Iran and the United States remained enemies after the Iran hostage crisis. Relations between the two nations have never recovered. The United States regards Iran as a dangerous nation that harbors terrorists. In 2002, U.S. president George W. Bush referred to Iran, along with Iraq and North Korea, as an "axis of evil." Today, the greatest American fear about Iran is that the nation is developing nuclear weapons that it could use against the United States or its allies.

instantly and bringing the building crashing to the ground. Sixty-three people were killed in the explosion. It was the deadliest terrorist attack against the United States at that time.

Hezbollah carried out an even deadlier attack six months later. A suicide bomber drove a truck into a U.S. Marine barracks at Beirut International Airport. It killed 241 U.S. Marines. A string of violent incidents followed. The U.S. Embassy in Kuwait was bombed later in 1983. And a number of embassies in Tehran were bombed in 1987. American CIA agent William Buckley was kidnapped in Lebanon in 1985. The kidnappers tortured Buckley, and he died in captivity. He was one of dozens of people kidnapped by terrorists in Lebanon from 1982 to 1992.

Terrorists also **hijacked** several commercial airplanes filled with passengers during these years. Some hijackings ended peacefully, but others ended in tragedy when passengers were killed. On December 21, 1988, terrorists planted a bomb on board Pan Am Flight 103. The bomb exploded as the plane was flying over Lockerbie, Scotland, carrying 259 people from London to New York. Everyone aboard was killed, and so were some people on the ground.

These and other attacks proved to terrorists that the United States could be hurt. Those who despised American influence in the world had discovered that they could wage war on Americans without fighting against the U.S. military.

The bombing of Flight 103 was a major tragedy.

CHAPTER 4

THE OKLAHOMA CITY BOMBING

The Oklahoma City bombing was one of the biggest terrorist attacks in U.S. history.

ON THE SUNNY MORNING OF April 19, 1995, thousands of people were arriving at work in the office buildings of downtown Oklahoma City, Oklahoma. In one horrifying moment, a massive bomb hidden in a truck exploded. It destroyed a government building. This is considered the first true terrorist attack to occur on American soil.

The Alfred P. Murrah Federal Building was home to many government offices.

Payback for Waco

Several divisions of the U.S. government had offices at the Alfred P. Murrah Federal Building, where the bomb went off. They included the Bureau of Alcohol, Tobacco, Firearms and Explosives (ATF) and the Federal Bureau of Investigation (FBI). The ATF and the FBI were the targets of this terrorist attack. But hundreds of innocent bystanders were caught in the destruction.

Events that had happened two years earlier played a part in this terrible attack. In 1993, an ATF raid on a religious cult called the Branch Davidians had turned disastrous. Cult leader David Koresh and his followers lived on a private ranch with several buildings, called a compound, in Waco, Texas. ATF agents attempted to take over the compound because they believed women and children were being mistreated there. But cult members fired back at the agents. The ATF could not gain control of the compound. The FBI stormed the compound after a 51-day standoff. A building where many cult members were hiding was burned. Koresh and 75 others died as the standoff came to a tragic end. As news of the disastrous raid spread around the

The building in Waco, Texas, where the cult members were hiding burned to the ground.

The Militia Movement

Many Americans who were angry at the U.S. government joined militia groups in the 1990s. Militia members sought greater freedoms to own weapons. They also wanted the government to stop interfering in individuals' lives. Many militia members were former U.S. military personnel who had left the armed services. They used their weapons knowledge and military experience in their plans for anti-government actions. Timothy McVeigh (above) and Terry Nichols attended several militia meetings. Although they shared the same beliefs as the militias, they never formally joined.

nation, Americans expressed shock over the many victims, who included children.

Conspirators' Plot

Timothy McVeigh was one of the many people who objected to the FBI's actions in Waco. McVeigh had joined the U.S. Army in 1988 when he was 20 years old. He served in the Persian Gulf War (1990–1991) and was discharged in 1991. In the army, McVeigh befriended a man named Terry Nichols. In 1993, the two men sat together in Nichols's home and watched with horror as the Waco siege played out on television. Waco only added to each man's unhappiness with the U.S. government.

McVeigh targeted the Oklahoma City federal building because he believed that the FBI office there had issued orders in the Waco siege. He and his group spent many months planning the bombing. McVeigh was the leader of the plot. He was assisted by Nichols, who had vast bomb-making expertise. They were joined by Michael Fortier, who was another army friend of McVeigh's, and his wife, Lori.

April 19, 1995

On the fateful morning, Timothy McVeigh found himself carrying out the plan alone. Terry Nichols had lost his nerve at the last minute. He had helped to build the bomb in the back of a rental truck. But he stayed home as McVeigh drove off to Oklahoma City. McVeigh parked in front of the Murrah Building just before 9:00 a.m.

Security camera footage shows the rental truck McVeigh used to bomb the Murrah Building.

The bomb caused massive damage to the Murrah Building and the surrounding area.

People were arriving for work. Adults weren't the only ones present. The building housed a day care center where workers were dropping off their children.

McVeigh lit the fuse to his bomb, got out of the truck, and walked away. He walked slowly at first so he wouldn't look suspicious. Then he started running because he knew how powerful the bomb was.

The bomb exploded at 9:02 a.m. It sent a shock wave through downtown Oklahoma City. People felt the blast 6 miles (10 kilometers) away.

McVeigh himself was knocked to the ground by the blast. He got up and ran to his getaway car, which he had parked on a street several days earlier. But McVeigh didn't get very far. About an hour after the bomb went off, he was pulled over by an Oklahoma state trooper because his car did not have proper license plate tags. The trooper found a concealed gun in the car and arrested him.

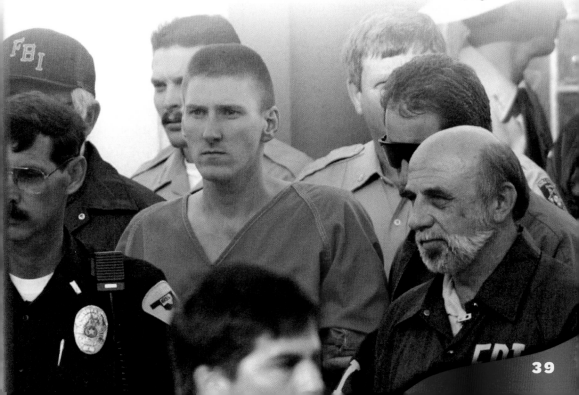

Timothy McVeigh was arrested soon after the bombing.

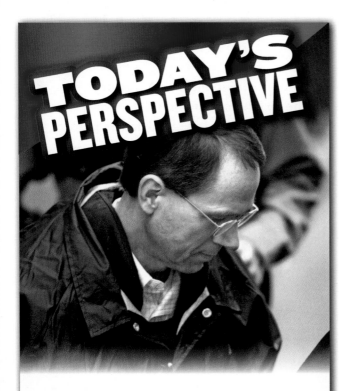

TODAY'S PERSPECTIVE

New evidence surfaced about Timothy McVeigh's role in the Oklahoma City bombing more than a decade after the bombing. Terry Nichols (above) was interviewed in prison in 2005. For the first time, he claimed that another person played a major role in planning the attack. But he would not name that person. The report on this interview was made public in 2011. Some terrorism experts now believe that McVeigh and Nichols actually worked with a terror network based outside the United States.

The devastation at the Murrah Building was immense. Some people died instantly from the blast. Many more perished as a large portion of the building collapsed in a massive pile of rubble. At that time, it was the deadliest terrorist attack ever on U.S. soil. It killed 168 people, including 19 children.

Trial and Punishment

Law enforcement officials were lucky to capture Timothy McVeigh as he fled Oklahoma City. From that point on, it was easy to piece together a case against the Oklahoma City bombers. Michael Fortier testified against McVeigh and Terry Nichols. He was sentenced to 12 years in prison. Lori Fortier also

People across the country paid close attention to McVeigh's trial.

testified against them but was not sentenced to any jail time. Nichols received a sentence of life in prison.

McVeigh, who single-handedly set off the bomb, was sentenced to death. On June 11, 2001, he was executed at a federal prison in Indiana. Exactly three months later, another group of terrorists would unleash the single most devastating attack in American history.

CHAPTER 5

SEPTEMBER 11, 2001

The World Trade Center was one of the most recognizable landmarks in New York City.

NOBODY KNOWS HOW MANY
terrorist plots against the United States have failed. Failed terror plots are rarely reported on the news. Timing, luck, and many other factors are needed for a foreign terrorist group to successfully launch a major attack within U.S. borders. American law enforcement had succeeded for many years in blocking terrorists from penetrating U.S. security. On September 11, 2001, terrorists were finally able to break through these defenses.

The 1993 World Trade Center bombing caused damage but did not destroy the buildings.

The Terrorists

The 9/11 attacks were planned and carried out by the terrorist group al-Qaeda. Al-Qaeda is an Islamist group that seeks jihad, or holy war, with certain non-Muslim nations. For years, the group attacked U.S. targets such as embassies. In 2000, al-Qaeda bombed the USS *Cole,* an American naval ship, killing 17 American sailors. Al-Qaeda also had connections to a bombing at the World Trade Center in 1993. In this incident, terrorists set off a truck bomb in an underground garage beneath the

North Tower. It killed six people. One of the bombers had trained with al-Qaeda. The organization's founder, Osama bin Laden, had helped fund the attack.

As early as 1996, al-Qaeda member Khalid Sheikh Mohammed was planning a complex terrorist attack on the United States. By 2001, bin Laden had approved Mohammed's plan to attack several symbolic U.S. structures.

SPOTLIGHT ON

Osama bin Laden

Osama bin Laden was born into a wealthy family in Saudi Arabia in 1957. As a young man, bin Laden joined the effort to fight the Soviet Union's 1979 invasion of the Muslim nation of Afghanistan. This began his lifelong commitment to defending strict Islamist rule in Muslim countries. He led the al-Qaeda terrorist network for decades before the U.S. military killed him in 2011.

Al-Qaeda knew that to succeed in such a plan, it would need a powerful new way to cause destruction. It decided that commercial airplanes loaded with fuel would work better than bombs.

Hijackers Take Control

Nineteen al-Qaeda terrorists boarded four different airplanes on the morning of September 11, 2001. Two planes took off from Boston, Massachusetts, one from Washington, D.C., and the fourth from Newark, New Jersey. The flights were all headed for the West Coast.

The hijackers were led by Mohamed Atta.

Each aircraft carried a large amount of jet fuel for the long journey. They were four massive missiles.

The hijackers took control of the aircraft almost immediately after the flights took off. They did not bring guns or other weapons on board because they would have been discovered by airport security. They instead used ordinary objects such as small, razor-sharp box cutters. Once the hijackers entered the cockpits of the aircraft, they likely killed the flight crew and took over the controls. Each plane suddenly turned off its course and headed for either New York City or Washington, D.C.

A FIRSTHAND LOOK AT
THE FLIGHT RECORDINGS

As Boston air traffic controllers sat in bewilderment at the radio silence from two aircraft that had recently taken off, a voice suddenly came through from American Airlines Flight 11. Someone had turned on the radio, broadcasting the words that the hijackers were telling the passengers. See page 60 for a link to read an online transcript of that broadcast and the one from United Flight 175.

Three of the planes reached their targets. But one did not. Cell phone conversations revealed that passengers aboard United Airlines Flight 93 bravely fought the terrorists on board. They stormed the cockpit and caused the pilot to crash the plane in an empty field in Pennsylvania. They sacrificed their own lives to save many more.

Flight 93 crashed in a field near Shanksville, Pennsylvania.

Witnesses were shocked to see planes collide with the Twin Towers of the World Trade Center.

The Twin Towers Are Struck

At 8:46 a.m., American Airlines Flight 11 crashed into the North Tower of the World Trade Center. Immediately, a massive fireball of jet fuel ignited. It instantly killed all passengers aboard and many people inside the building. Most people on the ground had no idea that it was a terrorist attack. Vice President Dick Cheney remembers being puzzled as he watched the North Tower fire on television, thinking "It was a clear day, there was no weather problem—how . . . could a plane hit the World Trade Center?"

United Airlines Flight 175 streaked across the New York skyline seventeen minutes later. It crashed into the South Tower at 9:03. It immediately became clear that this was not an accident. The United States was under attack.

A massive rescue effort took place in the next hour. Office workers streamed out of the two towers and filled the streets of lower Manhattan. But then the nightmare became even worse. Weakened from the intense heat of the fires, the South Tower's supporting structure gave way. The top floors fell into the floors below, and the entire building collapsed in a matter of seconds. By this time, television cameras were fixed on the burning towers, broadcasting live images around the world. Just a half hour later, the North Tower collapsed as well. On the streets of Manhattan, thousands of panicked people fled from the destruction.

People near the World Trade Center fled from clouds of dust and debris.

The disaster worsened when the Pentagon was attacked.

The Pentagon Is Attacked

As the tragedy in New York unfolded, government officials realized the hijackings and crashes were a coordinated attack. When American Airlines Flight 77 appeared to set its course for the nation's capital, the military began preparing for the worst. Most people assumed the plane would strike the White House. Instead, the aircraft flew to nearby Arlington, Virginia, and crashed into the west wall of the Pentagon. All 64 people on board were killed. So were 125 people on the ground. The death toll could have easily been higher. More than 25,000 people work at the Pentagon. Had the plane crashed in a more central part of the building, it would have done even greater damage.

A Day of Tragedy

Panic and fear filled the rest of the day. The military went into high alert. They assumed that additional threats would arise. All airline flights were canceled, and all planes in the air were ordered to land. Citizens everywhere struggled with the fear that terrorists

A VIEW FROM ABROAD

Reactions to the 9/11 attacks were divided in Muslim nations. Libyan president Muammar Qaddafi said that Muslim groups should help the United States "regardless of political considerations or differences between America and the peoples of the world."

In Iraq, which had been at war with the United States in recent years, the September 12 headline of the official government newspaper read "America Burns." The story stated that "the American cowboys are reaping the fruit of their crimes against humanity."

could strike again without warning. Rescue efforts continued at the Pentagon and the World Trade Center. Approximately 3,000 people lost their lives on September 11, and many thousands more were injured. It was a day of tragedy that the world will never forget.

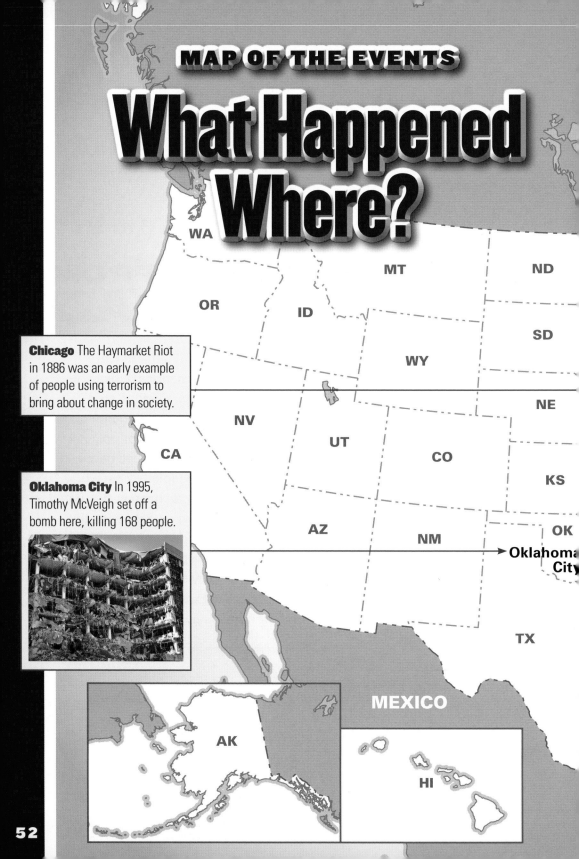

MAP OF THE EVENTS

What Happened Where?

WA

MT

ND

OR

ID

SD

WY

Chicago The Haymarket Riot in 1886 was an early example of people using terrorism to bring about change in society.

NE

NV

UT

CA

CO

KS

Oklahoma City In 1995, Timothy McVeigh set off a bomb here, killing 168 people.

AZ

NM

OK

Oklahoma City

TX

MEXICO

AK

HI

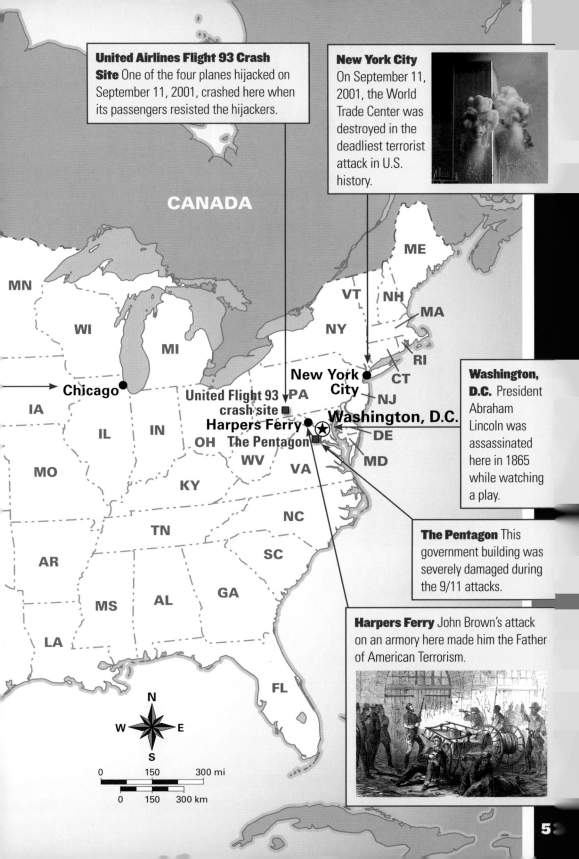

United Airlines Flight 93 Crash Site One of the four planes hijacked on September 11, 2001, crashed here when its passengers resisted the hijackers.

New York City On September 11, 2001, the World Trade Center was destroyed in the deadliest terrorist attack in U.S. history.

CANADA

Washington, D.C. President Abraham Lincoln was assassinated here in 1865 while watching a play.

The Pentagon This government building was severely damaged during the 9/11 attacks.

Harpers Ferry John Brown's attack on an armory here made him the Father of American Terrorism.

MN
WI
MI
IA
Chicago
IL
IN
OH
MO
KY
AR
TN
MS
AL
GA
LA
FL

ME
VT
NH
MA
NY
RI
CT
NJ
PA
United Flight 93 crash site
New York City
Harpers Ferry
Washington, D.C.
The Pentagon
DE
MD
WV
VA
NC
SC

N
W   E
S

0   150   300 mi
0   150   300 km

The War on Terror

The U.S. military has spent many years fighting terrorists in Afghanistan.

Terrorism has changed the United States in many ways. Immediately following 9/11, the U.S. government took measures to guard against terrorists reaching America. President George W. Bush signed the USA Patriot Act into law on October 26, 2001. It allowed law enforcement more freedom to spy on people suspected of being terrorists. Security grew tighter at the country's borders as the government attempted to stop potential terrorists from entering.

Critics of these measures complained that the government was protecting citizens by taking away their individual rights. The government argued that in a time of war, the extra measures were necessary.

President Bush declared a "war on terror" on September 16, 2001. U.S. forces and their allies entered Afghanistan in October 2001 to root out terrorist groups such as al-Qaeda. They also hunted for Osama bin Laden. But for many years he managed to stay hidden. Finally, in 2011, U.S. forces tracked him down in neighboring Pakistan and killed him. U.S. military involvement in Afghanistan continues.

War also broke out between the United States and Iraq, when the U.S. military attempted to find weapons of mass destruction that were believed to be stored there. No such weapons were ever found.

It is difficult to find a long period of peace in U.S. history. The nation has been involved in many armed conflicts since its founding. For the most part, the United States has fought wars only in foreign lands. This allowed Americans at home to maintain a sense of security. Terrorists have dealt a blow to that sense of security. Americans now know that terrorists—both American and foreign—can shatter peace in the United States.

INFLUENTIAL INDIVIDUALS

John Brown

John Brown (1800–1859) was an abolitionist who used violence against the U.S. government to try to end slavery.

John Wilkes Booth (1838–1865) was a supporter of the Confederacy and the assassin of Abraham Lincoln.

Luigi Galleani (1861–1931) was an Italian anarchist who launched bombings in the United States in the early 1900s.

Ayatollah Khomeini (1902–1989) was the religious leader and ruler of Iran who challenged the United States during the Iran hostage crisis.

Jimmy Carter (1924–) was the U.S. president who faced the Iran hostage crisis.

George W. Bush (1946–) was president of the United States at the time of 9/11.

Osama bin Laden (1957–2011) was the leader of the terrorist network al-Qaeda.

Osama bin Laden

Timothy McVeigh (1968–2001) was the leader of a small terrorist group that carried out the Oklahoma City bombing.

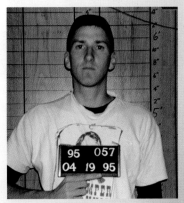

Timothy McVeigh

TIMELINE

1859

October 16
John Brown raids the federal arsenal in Harpers Ferry.

1861-1865

The American Civil War is fought.

1865

April 14
Abraham Lincoln is shot by John Wilkes Booth.

1979-1981

The Iran hostage crisis lasts 444 days.

1983

April 18
The U.S. Embassy in Beirut is bombed.

1988

December 21
Pan Am Flight 103 is blown up over Lockerbie, Scotland.

1886

May 4
The Haymarket Riot erupts over workers' rights.

1919-1920

The Palmer Raids lead to more than 500 deportations.

1920

September 16
Wall Street is bombed by anarchists.

1995

April 19
The Alfred P. Murrah Federal Building in Oklahoma City is bombed by Timothy McVeigh.

2001

September 11
Al-Qaeda carries out attacks on the World Trade Center and the Pentagon.

LIVING HISTORY

Primary sources provide firsthand evidence about a topic. Witnesses to a historical event create primary sources. They include autobiographies, newspaper reports of the time, oral histories, photographs, and memoirs. A secondary source analyzes primary sources, and is one step or more removed from the event. Secondary sources include textbooks, encyclopedias, and commentaries.

Barry Rosen Interview Barry Rosen was one of the 52 U.S. citizens held captive in Iran for 444 days from 1979 to 1981. You can read a transcript of his CNN interview by visiting *http://transcripts .cnn.com/TRANSCRIPTS/0601/20/lol.01.html*

Flight Recordings from 9/11 Audio recordings were broadcast from two of the hijacked planes on 9/11. You can view transcripts of the recordings by visiting *www.guardian.co.uk/world/2001/oct/17 /september11.usa*

Haymarket Flyers Flyers advertising the Haymarket meeting that turned into a massive riot can be viewed online. To see them, visit *http://en.wikipedia.org/wiki/File:Haymarketnewspaper.jpg* and *http:// en.wikipedia.org/wiki/File:Haymarket_Flier.jpg*

John Brown's Holy War John Brown's final letter and other interesting correspondence have been preserved as historical artifacts. You can read transcripts of some of his letters online by visiting *www.pbs.org/wgbh/amex/brown/filmmore/reference/primary /index.html*

Timothy McVeigh's Letters While he awaited execution on death row, Timothy McVeigh wrote several letters explaining why he bombed the Murrah Building in Oklahoma City. You can read the letters at *www.guardian.co.uk/world/2001/may/06/mcveigh.usa*

RESOURCES

Books

Benoit, Peter. *September 11: We Will Never Forget*. New York: Children's Press, 2012.

Fradin, Dennis Brindell. *The Assassination of Abraham Lincoln*. Tarrytown, NY: Marshall Cavendish Benchmark, 2007.

Horn, Geoffrey M. *John Brown: Putting Actions Above Words*. New York: Crabtree, 2010.

Landau, Elaine. *Suicide Bombers: Foot Soldiers of the Terrorist Movement*. Minneapolis: Twenty-First Century Books, 2007.

Marcovitz, Hal. *The Oklahoma City Bombing*. Philadelphia: Chelsea House, 2002.

Tougas, Shelley. *What Makes a Terrorist?* Mankato, MN: Compass Point Books, 2010.

Wachtel, Alan. *September 11: A Primary Source History*. Pleasantville, NY: Gareth Stevens, 2009.

Zeiger, Jennifer. *The War in Afghanistan*. New York: Children's Press, 2012.

Web Sites

FEMA: Terrorism
www.fema.gov/hazard/terrorism/index.shtm
Check out information from the Federal Emergency Management Agency (FEMA) about the nation's preparedness for terrorist attacks.

Homeland Security
www.dhs.gov/index.shtm
Read about the Department of Homeland Security, a federal government division that was formed in the aftermath of 9/11.

9/11 Memorial
www.national911memorial.org
Visit the official Web site for the 9/11 Memorial, being constructed on the site of the World Trade Center.

GLOSSARY

abolitionists (ab-uh-LISH-uh-nists) people in favor of immediately ending slavery

anarchists (AN-ar-kists) people who believe in lawlessness and want to bring down a country's government

assassinate (uh-SASS-uh-nate) to murder, usually someone well known

communists (KAHM-yuh-nistz) people who believe that all the land, property, business, and resources belong to the government or community and that the profits should be shared by all

deported (di-PORT-id) sent back to the country from which a person came

embargo (em-BAR-go) official order forbidding something from happening, especially trade

hijacked (HYE-jakd) forced an airplane pilot to surrender control of a plane

hostages (HOSS-tij-iz) innocent people who are taken captive and used as bargaining tools

labor movement (LAY-bur MOOV-muhnt) an organized struggle for workers' rights

suicide bomber (SOO-uh-side BOM-ur) a terrorist who intentionally dies in the explosion that he or she sets off

terrorists (TARE-ur-ists) people who attack governments or innocent people in order to disrupt society and create chaos

INDEX

Page numbers in *italics* indicate illustrations.

ABOUT THE AUTHOR

Mark Friedman has been a writer and editor of children's books and educational materials for 20 years. He has written books on history, politics, government, science, religion, and sports as well as textbooks and other classroom materials. Mark lives with his family near Chicago, Illinois.